This book is dedicated to my family , friends, and the many who inspired it.

ISBN: 1463705271
ISBN-13: 978-1463705275

Thoughts on Life

By Michael F. Ring

By taking different routes to your destination you'll discover the destination doesn't matter.

Helping others builds the spirit just as exercise builds the body.

A walk in the rain isn't a bad way to spend a rainy day.

God speaks to those who listen

The sun is always shining, whether we see it or not

Sharing is as important as giving.

*The cat purring next to
you is reminding you that
life is good!*

----

*Teachers use books to give
us knowledge.
God uses our experiences
to give us wisdom.
What we learn is up to us.*

Silence lets you hear God.

You don't need a lot of stuff to enjoy life.

Sometimes saying nothing is better than saying more than you should.

Empty waiting drains life from the soul

You don't need a reason to hug or love someone.

When someone takes the time to share with you something important to them, you should take the time to listen.

The best teacher is a child or a good student.

Appreciate each breath of fresh air.

Doing a good deed without reward is still doing a good deed.

Don't expect others to be nice to you if you aren't nice to them first.

Nothing is truly secret if you can guess what it is.

When you listen to God, you won't wonder what was said.

When cooking, don't be lazy or sloppy. The most memorable meals are those made with love and care.

Doing what is right is not always easy, but you will not regret it.

Things don't always work out the way we want, but that's good, because we'd be really spoiled if they did.

The best music is felt, not heard.

Do the words of a prophet change the future?

The path you are on does not only lead forward.

The most valuable education is that which you can use.

*The smile on your face is
a reflection of those
around you.*

----

*Enjoy the sunshine
because it warms your
face. Appreciate the rain
because it gives you life.
And love the world
because you are part of it.*

----

*The past should give us
wisdom and good
memories, nothing more.*

*True messages from God
are written within our
spirit if we choose to know
them.*

----

*Thanksgiving is
celebrated year-round by
those truly thankful.*

----

*Hard work is easier if you
enjoy it.*

The extra-ordinary person is an average person who decided to be different.

The smallest kindness is often the most appreciated.

When given a hug, don't forget to return it.

Share happiness, good fortune, and good memories.

Try to start the New Year like a new day, fresh, with love and a smile.

When leading, make a good path for those who will follow.

If a person has a closed mind, their ears and eyes do not matter and their mouth should remain closed too.

Remember to be there for those who are there for you.

Spring is best after a cold winter.

Don't ask if you can help... just help.

Life's most difficult decisions usually involve balancing now with what may happen later.

Patience is one's selflessness shared with yourself and others.

Sunday shopping and TV have replaced most Sunday dinners.

If man is so smart, why do we learn so much from God's creatures?

Sometimes angels need help finding you... help them by being an angel yourself.

*Step outside your own
limitations and you can
do anything.*

---

*Advice given by those
who care and repeated by
those who love is precious
and should be respected.*

---

*Only when you close your
eyes can you tell if your
pain is from within or
without.*

*The best words on a page
lead to powerful thoughts
in the mind.*

----

*Nothingness is as difficult
to comprehend as infinity.*

----

*Everything you do
becomes part of you.*

Never give up, but know when your effort is best used elsewhere.

Birds fly wherever there is air. Fish swim where there is water. We should appreciate what we can do.

You need own nothing if you give of yourself.

Sometimes it is better to simply move on than to try to figure out what happened

----

Notice what you are passing and be part of what is around you

----

Work hard, play hard, but don't forget to rest.

Thank those who help you
And help those who don't.

Adding spice to your life
only works when your
base recipe is good.

There's no need to count
your blessings when you
feel blessed.

Money can buy happiness when you give it away to someone who appreciates it.

What you do today may change what you can do tomorrow

Don't ask why you should do something... instead ask why not?

When you see everything
as black or white, you are
missing all the colors

You don't need money or
possessions to be a good
person.

Just because you can do
something doesn't mean
you should

When you look in the mirror, do you see your true self?

Don't build your life on your opinions.

Wisdom is knowledge combined with experience.

Live each day unselfishly.

----

*Saying I'll do it tomorrow
may stop you from
succeeding today.*

----

*When someone steps on
your toes, perhaps you
need to watch where you
are going.*

*Too much of a good thing
is probably a bad thing.*

----

*It isn't so much as what
you've learned, as it is
what you've done with it.*

----

*Remember the important
things.*

Love cannot exist without forgiveness

Start the day with a smile and happiness usually follows.

When you fall on your face, at least you can see where you landed.

*Children teach you
important things you
have forgotten.*

----

*A prayer does not need
words.*

----

*The wisest exhibit the
most patience.*

When you choose to do something, do not blame others for the result.

Follow the laughter to find happiness

Feel beautiful and be beautiful.

Don't assume people will do the right thing, but set an example anyway.

Youth should respect experience while age should respect new ideas.

Be who you are, not someone else.

*Good conversation makes
a good meal memorable.*

----

*To change your life, you
need to take a chance.*

----

*Remember that you are
one of God's creatures too.*

*Touch the mind and touch
the heart.*

---

*Your laughter should
bring smiles to those
around you.*

---

*Pride and Foolishness
walk hand in hand*

*Free will means you can
do what you want, but
not without consequences*

----

*A true friend will always
care and forgive.*

----

*Find a use for the clutter
in your life or get rid of it.*

If you keep doing the right thing, eventually good will come from it.

The truth in God's message does not require translation.

When you feel you can't go on, maybe it is time to change direction or take a break.

Today matters to someone.

You don't need an occasion to give someone a smile.

Cats are ticklish but have no sense of humor.

Not doing the wrong thing is not the same as doing the right thing, rather it is the same as doing nothing.

Always be thankful

Goodness and Mercy may follow you, but are best carried in your heart.

*The End can be a start to
a new beginning.*